CONTENTS

DIVINE ENCOUNTERS

Stories of God's goodness by an ordinary disciple

Roy Pearson

Dedicated to my beloved Gilly, a gift from God

I walk the paths we used to walk
Gaze upon scenes we loved to share
I see again your lovely face
Your radiant smile, your auburn hair
To me, just beautiful.

FOREWORD

Growing up as the youngest son of Roy and Gillian Pearson, I am in a better position than most to verify the God encounters written about in this book. In fact, I can go one better than that and add to them. There was never a dull moment with Mum and Dad – they immersed us into a life of "seeking the kingdom first" (Matthew 6v33) and modelled it in very real ways.

For instance, I recall as a teenager coming down the stairs with pain from a badly cricked neck. Dad came over to me, prayed briefly and put his hand on me. As he did, I was completely better. I can also remember a time when I tore a ligament playing football and when Mum prayed, I could feel power all around the ankle area where I was injured. It was like electricity, and though I wasn't completely healed there was a significant improvement after that. Then there was another time when I was at school and had lost my pencil case somewhere. I told Dad about it that evening and, a few moments later, he came out of the kitchen after having had a mental picture of the pencil case under a certain seat on the school coach. That next morning as I boarded the coach, I headed for the seat Dad had mentioned. It wasn't there, but another pupil told me that my pencil case had been in that exact spot and had been handed in to lost property!

Much later in life, when Mum was so ill with dementia, Dad and I were in waiting room in Southampton General hospital. Mum had, had a kind of seizure and fall. Dad had asked a whole load of friends to pray about the situation and as we sat there an overwhelming sense of peace came over us, despite what was going on. As we left to go home, Dad had to pay for parking at the hospital Pay on Exit machines. Searching through his wallet and pockets he realised he was short of cash for the full payment, but to our amazement the right amount - a 50 pence piece suddenly appeared in his hand! I cannot stress enough how strange this was to see; an empty hand one moment, then a coin suddenly appeared in it. I had read about Jesus telling Simon Peter to pay tax from a coin in a fish's mouth but this was the first time I had seen something appear from literally nowhere!

Looking back, I remember something that sums it all up for me – where we lived in Hedge End during the 1980s we had a garage at the end of the drive. It was filled up with bikes, beach stuff, the lawnmower, assorted junk, and some DIY stuff that none of us knew how to use! There were cluttered shelves and it wasn't exactly an organised space. Yet on one of the shelves, placed in a prominent position there was this white wooden sign with very 'olde worlde' style lettering in gold. It said, "Prayer changes things." Every time you walked into the garage those words would hit you. Mum and Dad really believed that. They prayed a lot and they believed that God would change things. I hope you will enjoy reading Dad's accounts and will that you will find out more and more yourself that, even in the busyness and chaos of our lives, which are sometimes as messy and disorganised as our old garage in Hedge End, that prayer really does change things.

Jamie Pearson

INTRODUCTION

Jesus came announcing a very specific message, 'the kingdom of God has come' (Matthew 4v17). Rather than proclaiming a future hope of heaven later, Jesus is making a dynamic declaration of immediacy! The kingdom of God is here now, acting in time and space, in human experience and this is what it looks like, this is what is real and present. That declaration could only be made with a harmonising of words and works. One simply cannot say it, without showing it. It would be like announcing 'electricity is here!' but never switching on a light to demonstrate that it is so.

How do we understand the kingdom of God? The dynamic reign of God is certainly a fantastic way to define it, but what has helped me in understanding the kingdom is to see it as God's love in action. Jesus came declaring and demonstrating God's love in action. His healings, miracles, setting people free from darkness and death, all reveal the compassion and mercy and power of God.

The following pages are my Dad's stories of God's love in action. The purpose of the book is not so much as to record his exploits but rather to inspire others that, in his own words, 'if I can do this, anyone can'. As I read the drafts of the book as we worked on it, I found myself encouraged to ask Jesus for a deeper revelation of Him and for more encounters with Him, and was also inspired again to give away to those around me whatever He gives me. I suspect reading it will do the same for you.

Dad has many more stories than included here, not just of God's love in action in healing and filling people, but also of God's Fatherly provision for His beloved children. Growing up we saw the provision of God in housing, finances, jobs and cars, plus, plus... The simple, childlike trust mum and dad lived out was all encompassing. That default expectation of God's kind involvement in our lives is a wonderful legacy to leave kids and grandkids, even, one day, great grandkids!

So, with heartfelt thanks to Dad and Mum, let me introduce these stories by Roy Pearson.

Mike Pearson

CHAPTER ONE:
MY JOURNEY

It was a Saturday morning in the autumn of 1949. I was 10 years of age. I had called for my friend Brian, who lived in Dimond Road, just ten minutes walk from my home. Along with others, Brian and I had a great time playing in a large open area of ground known as the Brickfields. We built camps, racetracks, hideouts and adventure trails in this huge site that had formerly been a smallholding and brickworks. This area is now covered by Bitterne Park School and Sixth-Form College. That morning Brian could not come out until he had finished his household chores, so I waited patiently for him across the road from his home. I waited for perhaps 10-15 minutes there.

There was a strong wind blowing that day, and up towards the hills of Midanbury it was beginning to make a loud howling noise, not unusual for that place or time. But I was there alone and gave some thought to it, as I had little else to do. I thought, "How strong God must be to control the wind and the waves". I recalled this from Sunday school Bible stories and from children's choruses we sang. Suddenly it was as though someone spoke to me from behind, or was it from above? "Yes, I am strong and I am right here with you". I was not afraid but astonished, and I recall looking around and wondering, "Who was that? Where is that voice coming from?" Then it began to dawn on me – could it be God himself? But why me, and what does it all mean? I knew that day, aged 10, that God was real and so very close.

I made a definite commitment to follow Jesus at the age of 14. I had attended a Youth for Christ rally, at what was then the Methodist Central Hall in St Marys in Southampton. A Christian film produced by the Billy Graham Evangelistic Association called "Oil Town" was shown on a big screen and I knew I wanted to go forward at the end of the message. My life began to change significantly. I was a member of Bitterne Park Baptist church and got involved in leading the Boys Brigade and a Bible class of 50 young people.

Bitterne Park has always been a special place for me. I was born in 36 Oaktree Road. My beloved Gillian lived at 79 Oaktree Road. We first met at a bus stop in that same road and arranged to meet that evening for a walk at Riverside Park. I had never been out with a girl before. What a wonderful surprise I had! We had walked only 20 yards down Wellington Road when Gillian took my hand as we continued together towards the park. Months later I mentioned this to her, joking that she was very quick off the mark! Gillian replied, "Well, I knew straight away that you were my husband, so why hold back?" She was fourteen years old, whilst I was sixteen. Within weeks we had fallen head over heels in love and I proposed to her in the front room of her home, with her dear Mum and Dad in the next room. She said, "Yes, but I won't be able to leave Mum and Dad just yet!" We waited 6 years, getting married on 3rd March 1962. It was a great day (incredibly the Saints soccer team beat Scunthorpe at the Dell 6-4!!).

Gillian never really left her mum because we moved into a newly built bungalow in Ashtree Road, Bitterne Park. Its garden adjoined her parent's garden and the plot there was formerly her uncle's allotment. This too was a remarkable story that had the hand of God upon it. In 1950 new building sites were springing up all over Southampton, replacing open land and bombsites. The local brickworks in Dimond Road was run down and eventually closed. It was a wonderful playground full of fields, trees, bushes, camps and cycle tracks. It was a superb, open space where large numbers of children could play happily for hours.

One day my school pals noticed official notices fixed to the lamp-posts declaring that Southampton City Council had purchased the whole site for a new school! I walked home that evening with school pal Ken, who lived at up the road, and we talked about the loss of 'our' Brickfield.

Ken said, "They are building everywhere now. They will even build on this allotment one day".

I replied, "Well, I would like to live there if they do build homes on it". That was the summer of 1950. Twelve years later, in June 1962, Gillian and I moved into our newly built bungalow at 82 Ashtree Road, on that very spot where the allotment had been! We lived in that house almost 20 years, and our three children Mike, Julie and Jamie grew up there.

The Holy Spirit Moves
That was a home in Ash Tree Road that God used to bless many others. We had many home group meetings there where we worshipped for hours. We also had many visiting leaders and teachers who ministered in our home. People like James McConnell from Northern Ireland, Tony Stone (International evangelist), Arthur Wallis (International teacher and author), the prophetic David Mansell and apostolic Bryn Jones. These names might be unfamiliar to many of you, but were really significant for those of us at the time. They were all instrumental in the early charismatic movement in the UK during the 1960s, 70s and 80s.

Funnily enough, the old Brickfield I used to play in became a large school and during 1977-8 our church met there in the main hall, with over two hundred and fifty attending. Later, we moved on to the university's Boldrewood lecture hall in Bassett as the church grew to over 400. In the 1990s the church grew to 1000 and other churches were planted out, whilst men and women travelled all over the world sharing about the Kingdom of God.

Now, at 81 years old, I look back and see how God has been so good, so faithful. He gave me wonderful, loving parents and a good family, a beautiful wife who was so full of God and full of life (no one is perfect, but Gilly came very close!). I thank Him too for my three children and seven grandchildren, all of which are following Jesus.

During these years God has also shown me many precious things about His love and His care. I have been privileged to witness some glorious things, seeing dear people encounter Jesus and follow Him, them being filled with his Holy Spirit, healed, restored and set free.

His stories

I love to tell these 'God stories' to my family and friends. That is exactly what they are – His stories, not mine. Many people have encouraged me to write them down and pass them down to bless, encourage and inspire others in the days to come. Indeed, my children and grandchildren have already seen and experienced many precious times where God has used them, beyond my experiences, to see other dear people touched and blessed by God. So, as I recall and relate just some of these stories, let me emphasise again, these are God's stories, not mine. If I can do these things, anyone can! To Him be all the glory. I am a very ordinary man with an amazing God!

CHAPTER TWO: BEGINNING TO SEE PEOPLE ENCOUNTER JESUS

In John 1 v 29 we read, "John saw Jesus coming toward him and said, "Look, the Lamb of God who takes away the sin of the world". The sin of the world is separation from God and Jesus came to end that separation. He paid the price of our sin, ended our separation, bringing us into the family of God. Through His death at Calvary, He gave us life: a lifetime and eternity as children of God.

I first heard this wonderful truth at Sunday school. The Sunday school was packed with 40 to 50 of us kids gathered to learn about Jesus and to worship him in song. One of the first songs I can recall is "I will make you fishers of men". We sang it over and over again, louder and louder. One new boy went home at the end telling his parents he had sung a song about making us vicious old men! They soon learned the truth!

It became natural for me to tell people about Jesus. One day I shared at our young people's Bible class on John 3v16, 'For God so loved the world that He gave His only begotten son, that whosoever believes in Him will not perish but have eternal life.' That day, 4 young people came to Jesus and are still walking with Him all these years later; two of them are in church leadership. In the following months and years this became a regular occurrence with many teenage girls and boys coming to know Jesus. It is our assignment here on earth to know Jesus and share His love with others.

The following are stories of people being encountered by Jesus, as I did my best to obediently take the opportunities that He gave me.

Throughout this book many of the names have been changed.

A life transformed

During our time at Bitterne Park Baptist every Christmas, Easter and Harvest we would do what they called a "visitation" and would go in two's, to knock doors and invite people to our services.

We knocked at one door and began speaking to a man who said that he was not interested in attending, however he said "but we do have my niece here, and you can take her to Sunday school". Mary was eleven when we first met her at Bitterne Park. Her mother had died when she was very young and her Dad had remarried and she had had to relocate to go and live with her Grandad and uncle in Bitterne Park. Her young life had been full of challenges for some time.

Mary became a much-loved member of our youth organisation and Bible class and she began to follow Jesus. People in the church made a huge fuss of her. Later in the early 1970 she was one of the first to be baptised in the Holy Spirit and began to sing beautifully in a heavenly language. When she did so, she sang out powerfully like an opera singer in tongues. She changed dramatically as a person from being this shy, retiring girl to a bold witness. Mary became a superb teacher and then a headmistress, continuing now to serve as a church leader with her husband and their lovely daughter.

An angelic visitation
James was also a member of our youth work. At the age of 11 he accidentally found his own adoption papers at home. This affected him badly and he behaved very erratically. His problems continued as he got older and he ended up in Winchester Prison youth wing with a six-month sentence.

I felt I should visit him in prison, something I had never experienced before. It was all arranged and I sat opposite James in a large hall, filled with young men and their prison warders. I couldn't believe all these young men were offenders. With the prison warder standing right next to us, I encouraged James to give himself to God and to ask for forgiveness and the power to break free from the way of life he was trapped in. James asked Jesus into his heart and asked for forgiveness. It was a wonderful experience. I felt elated, so grateful and privileged to see this happen.

Five days later, to my great surprise, James turned up at my front door! "I've got so much to tell you", he said excitedly. "Can I come in?" James told us exactly what had happened that evening at Winchester prison, after I had left him there. He was asleep in his top bunk, with another prisoner below. Suddenly the room filled with light and James sat up to find an angel in his cell, surrounded by a bright light. He called James by name and he got up and knelt before the angel, overwhelmed by the situation. The angel spoke to him: "You prayed today for salvation and forgiveness but did not really pray from your heart but as a token gesture because your friend Roy had come to the prison to help you". James confirmed it was true, how could he hide anything from this angel who appeared to know all about him? "Now, James", he said, "if you truly mean it now, I want you to pray again, here with me". James did just that and the angel turned around and walked through the closed door! The cell became dark again. James could hardly believe this had happened – and his cellmate slept through it all!

Three days later James was summoned to the Prison Governor's office. The Governor told him that they felt James had experienced the shock of prison and would be set free on licence. However, he would have to pay a fine of £500!

James could not believe all that was happening to him so suddenly. That's when he arrived at our home. We were all so excited. We prayed that he would get a job to help him pay off the large fine. A couple of days later James was employed in the Fawley area working on the new construction site of an oil refinery. It was hard work and long hours but the pay was excellent. The fine was paid off in 6 months and James was never in trouble again. He later met and married a young lady who was also following Jesus and they served in a church in Southampton.

Didn't Jesus say he had come to set the prisoners free?

God at Work
For me the workplace was always a fruitful place to talk to people about God's love. One summer a young woman came to work in our office for the summer vacation. Anne attended university in Birmingham but lived in Southampton. I gave her a booklet one day called 'Journey into Life'. I gave them out to dozens of people. It was a clear but simple explanation of the gospel. She took it away to read. She was an extremely intelligent and very articulate person, and to my great surprise, she handed me the booklet back three days later and told me that she had prayed the prayer at the end of the booklet.

Two weeks later, at the local Pentecostal church, Anne experienced a powerful filling with the Holy Spirit and became on fire for God. The change in her life was so radical and amazing her parents asked to see my wife and I. They were quite alarmed at the change in Anne's life. They were pleased, but concerned that it might affect her studies at university! It didn't! Anne went on to gain a first-class degree with honours.

Wherever Peter went God was there!

Although some people respond quickly to the gospel, others may take a while, even years. Peter worked with me for the City Council as a probation officer. He lived nearby us and often visited our home. I shared about Jesus with him but he could not make the step of faith, in fact he found it hard to commit to any relationship.

Later he moved to Canada, 5 years later to New Zealand and eventually to Australia! After 10 years away from the UK, Peter returned home and bumped straight into me at Riverside Park one summer evening. He recalled, "Wherever I went I found God waiting for me! In Canada he found himself working with Christians. In New Zealand he moved into a town experiencing a revival with its local church packed. Then, in Australia, a work colleague "wouldn't stop talking about God". Peter came home still thinking over all that had happened to him and everything we had shared with him. He started coming to our church, gave himself to Jesus and was baptised. He had a great singing voice and loved to worship. It took 10 years of encounters with Jesus before he fully responded. Peter is now with Jesus in heaven.

Healings at work

I worked for over 34 years in the Social Services Department of Hampshire County Council and Southampton City Council. At one point I was working in the area office in Archers Road. I used to go into the office at 7:30am, partly to miss the rush hour traffic, but mainly to have a half hour of prayer whilst the place was empty and quiet.

One of our senior officers there was a tall, smartly dressed man with a heart of gold. Early one morning he stopped at my door and asked if he could join in with my prayer time! He was a Roman Catholic worshipper of God. He joined in and we became close friends. John had chronic back trouble following a serious accident some years before, that left him with a limp and one leg shorter than the other. The very first time we prayed John got healed! His leg grew instantly and he experienced no more pain whatsoever. Shortly after this he was filled to overflowing with the Holy Spirit. He shared all this at his church after which he was asked to speak at the next Catholic retreat!

One morning he brought along another Catholic friend, Janet, who was an experienced social worker. Janet had the early stages of cancer. John and I prayed for her four times in our prayer times together and she was healed. Janet told her local priest everything that had happened and he was really enthusiastic to hear all that had taken place with her and John. The priest invited her to accompany him three months later to pray for one of his church members who had stomach cancer. They prayed faithfully and God wonderfully healed the man completely!

A son and mother turn to Jesus

During my many years serving with local church youth organisations I frequently met with parents who asked a lot of questions. Colin was 14 years old. He came to Bible class regularly then requested a visit to his home. He wanted to enquire about becoming a Christian but preferred to talk to me privately at home. When I turned up at his house, I also met Colin's mum who insisted on listening to our discussion. After some explanation of the Bible, then questions from Colin, a very precious thing took place. Colin was keen to proceed, he had made up his mind, wanted to follow Jesus and was ready now to pray, but to my great surprise his mum said, "I've listened to all you had to say, I've been to church many times, but I have never taken that step of faith – I'd like to do it now!" So, we all knelt down and prayed. I later learned that my Gilly's sister, Teresa, had been sharing God's love with Colin's mum and praying for her for months.

CHAPTER THREE: YOU WILL RECEIVE POWER FROM ON HIGH

John the Baptist said, "I baptise you with water for repentance. But after me comes one who is more powerful than I, whose sandals I am not worthy to carry. He will baptise you with the Holy Spirit and fire". Matthew 3:11.

Jesus' last words to his closest friends were "Do not leave Jerusalem, but wait for the gift my Father promised… in a few days you will be baptised with the Holy Spirit." Luke 24v48.

In the early 1960s, Gillian and I were active members of our local Baptist church – it was not unusual for us to be out 3 or 4 times a week with church activities. By the time I was 26 years old I was a Deacon in the church and Gillian was the secretary of the Women's Contact group. We also served in the youth Bible class with over 50 members.

We had developed a great friendship with our Minister at the time – a young man called Derek and one day Derek lent us a book he had been reading. The book, called "The Cross and the Switchblade". It was the story of David Wilkerson and his efforts to reach out to gangs in New York City. In the book there was a whole chapter on being filled with the Holy Spirit which, he explained, led him to becoming much more effective in reaching out to people.

I was very interested in this and asked Derek about it, but he said that "We don't preach that in the Baptist church". However, I was determined to find out more and the longing of my heart was to see the empowering of the Holy Spirit that Wilkerson had described in his book.

As time went on, we became more and more convinced that the empowering of the Holy Spirit was what we needed, and this finally led to one Sunday evening in March 1971 when our lives were dramatically changed. We had hosted a meeting in our home for a group of teenagers from the church and when they all went home Gillian, then 7 months pregnant with our 3rd child, had gone to bed. I knelt down to pray in the lounge and give thanks to God for the day and to pray for the teenagers and our lovely family. I had been praying for barely five minutes when a wonderful immersion of love and warmth enveloped me and without any prompting or expectation, I began to praise God in another language. It was as if all heaven broke loose! It was wonderful, I felt pure, ecstatic joy, and looking around me in our lounge it was as though the whole room was bathed in a golden glow – the room was filled with the presence of God!

I rushed into our bedroom and tried to explain to Gillian what had happened. There was no holding her! She hurried to the lounge and knelt where I had knelt, thinking that surely God must still be there! He was – Gillian at once broke out in a beautiful language and experienced that same baptism in the Spirit. We were overwhelmed with God's love and continued in praise and worship and adoration until midnight!

Around that time, all over Britain, people in churches were experiencing the same thing and many of them, including us, were asked to leave those churches as their denominations either didn't understand at the time what was happening or disagreed with it. So we joined Millbrook Pentecostal Church for a season and on one morning new members of the congregation were

21

asked to stand up. Twenty-eight people stood up, all of them had been filled with the Holy Spirit and had been compelled to leave their churches.

What was happening was a sovereign and spontaneous work of God where people became very hungry for more of God than they had previously had. Several years before this, apostolic leader Bryn Jones had attended a Bible school in Wales at a centre, run by an intercessor named Rees Howells. In one of the regular three hour prayer sessions held at the centre, Bryn saw a vision of fires being ignited all over Britain. The fires all joined together and the flame of God engulfed the nation.

While Bryn was seeing this, he spoke aloud in tongues. After the session an Ethiopian lady caught up with him and started talking to him in a language he didn't understand. Suddenly realising Bryn didn't understand what she was saying, the Ethiopian spoke to him in English, saying "You were just speaking in Ethiopian, in fact in the very unique dialect of my village! You spoke about the fires of God all across Britain that would cover the nation and the rains of God that would bring restoration and revival!"

In 1973 Bryn Jones stayed at our home. We had shared with him our vision of a Spirit-filled house group/church along the same lines of the large church he led in Bradford. Bryn prayed with us before he left and prophesied, "I have seen the hunger in your hearts, the longing for more of my Kingdom. I will build my church here and I will add to you many who are hungry for my presence. Many more who you do not yet know, and many others who are not yet in my Kingdom."

What a faithful God we have. What started out as Southampton Christian Fellowship and went on to become the New Community Church, was established in February 1975 in the home of our close friends Rodney and Edna Martin.

I especially remember one men's meeting there. Rodney was going to lead about twelve of us in worship, but while he was tuning up and practising one song, God's presence came so powerfully that no one could stand up! My friend, Mike Evans, was the first to go down on the floor, followed by Rodney and several others. Several tried to get up from the floor only to receive more, and down again they went! I tried to explain what I thought was happening, but ended up under the sofa! It seemed to go on and on. Some laughed, some cried, it was just pure joy in God's presence. We were never the same again.

The Filling Station

The experience of being filled with the Spirit radically altered our spiritual life. We found a great release in worship and praise, both in the church at meetings and at home. That longing in our hearts for a closer relationship with God was met and we couldn't wait to get into the presence of God in worship. Soon we were given our first worship tapes and we filled our home with worship music. Our prayer life also changed dramatically from fairly quiet, formal prayers to a new level of adoration and fervent intercession. Those around us noticed this significant change in us and whilst some were encouraged, others were astonished and warned us of Pentecostal extremism! Our love of the Bible became stronger and its truths felt more fully alive to us. There was also a new boldness in evangelism and soon after our baptism in the Spirit we saw more people come to Christ.

We also began to see people get healed or filled with the Holy Spirit for the first time when we prayed for them. During an 18-month period in 1971 and 1972 over a hundred people came to Christ, were filled with the Spirit or were healed, all in our home. After a hundred people, we lost count – I believe the number was probably more like one hundred and fifty. A friend of ours who regularly brought his friends to be filled with the Holy Spirit renamed our home "The filling station".

Once a lady in her 30s arrived at our house desperate for a touch from God. Within 5 minutes she was immersed in the Holy Spirit and fell to the ground, prayed in a heavenly language and then burst into uncontrollable laughter and joy. The next day she came back and said that God had healed her from large varicose veins behind both her knees. Gillian and I hadn't even prayed for healing, not knowing about her condition!

People would turn up at our home often in twos', three's and four's, requesting prayer. Sometimes they would come in the day or in the evenings and there were people we had never met before, who had simply heard what had happened to us or to their friends. For example, one night four young nurses in uniform arrived. We explained from the Bible about the anointing of the Holy Spirit and then they knelt down to pray. Hardly had their knees reached the carpet when all were filled with the Spirit at once and worshipped in heavenly languages. Their joy was plain to see and was overwhelming.

It was during that time that the first of our 'childless couples' came along and received healing. Two couples known from my work asked for prayer. Both couples had been married several years and had been told by specialists and doctors that they would never be able to have children. In both cases God had other plans and the healing power of Jesus brought children into the world. Another evening a middle-aged man named Don arrived at our home. He was working in the Southampton area for 6 months. He lived in Cheshire and led a traditional church of about a hundred people. He had heard about what God had been doing and we explained about the filling of the Holy Spirit. Within minutes he was on the floor and praising God in tongues. We kept in touch with Don for months after and found out that after his visit to our home he had called his church leadership team together and had prayed for them. All of them were baptised in the Holy Spirit. That following Sunday night at church Don and his team spoke about what they had experienced and about 80% of his congregation were filled with the Holy Spirit. Within weeks the whole congregation received the Holy Spirit and there was an outbreak of healings and people becoming Christians.

Tom

Early in the 1980s I was asked by the leader of the Southampton Community Church to visit a man, I'll call him Tom Bailey, in the New Forest. This man was not a believer and his brother, up in Norfolk, was very concerned about him and asked if someone could visit him. We were told that this man was in his 60s and had had a very troubled life and had been in prison several times. More recently, his wife had died and so he was living alone in the New Forest, far from his family.

So, Gilly and I went down on a Sunday afternoon to see if we could help him. Though Tom was pleased to have a visit he was not enthused about Christianity. He just
wanted to talk about all the mistakes he had made in life and how he had been in prison and that his wife had died and how he lived far from his family. The first half an hour was really hard going! But then suddenly he explained how his mum had been a very active Methodist believer and that she told him that she had prayed for him every day for forty years.

I said, "Well, that changes the whole thing, Tom! If God has been hearing your name every day for forty years, then He is going to be on your case! He is going to help you." With that Tom sank to his knees and started singing old Methodist hymns very loudly! With "To God be the glory" echoing in the room, my faith began to rise, and I said, "Tom, God can change your life completely!" I led him in a prayer to know Jesus and receive what Jesus had done for him on the cross and to give his life to him. He prayed loudly and enthusiastically as he knelt on the floor. Everything changed for Tom. He was like a different man.

Before we left, Gilly and I encouraged him to read the Bible his wife had given him. We also linked him up with the New Forest church and we heard that several men from the church had visited him and were encouraging him.

Six weeks later we were at a gathering at Boldrewood university campus for a worship meeting and, to my amazement, among a group who had come along from the New Forest was Tom! He was lifting his hands and really worshipping and his face had a glow about it.

I spoke to him afterwards, and he said how he had felt like a different person after we had gone, but it was the next day that even more happened. He described how he had got up the next morning, opened the curtains and as the sunlight came in, power flowed into his chest and he fell down on the carpet. "God knocked me over!" he said, "Joy and peace poured into my heart. I have never felt anything like it!" He was so changed and also felt so loved and included by the New Forest church, that he was going round mending lawn mowers and cutting grass and serving people.

Tom continued to grow in his walk with Jesus over the next few weeks and then, six months later, I was told that he had, had visits from his family from Norfolk who were so amazed at his transformation that they asked him to return to live with them, which he did. God transformed this man's life and restored him to his family.

CHAPTER FOUR: THE COMMUNITY CHURCH AT HEDGE END

In 1981 Gillian and I moved to Hedge End to help establish a new Community Church there. I spent many hours walking the streets, praying for the area and distributing leaflets. One man gave his literature back retorting angrily, "We don't want another church here; we have 5 already and they are all half empty". God proved him wrong, Hedge End village grew to a town of 20,000 people, the church we helped to plant with 20 people eventually grew to 800 and continues to thrive today, planting out churches in other areas.

In a ten-month period during 1984 and 1985 forty-three people became followers of Jesus as the Holy Spirit was at work with us. Many others were healed, set free from things that oppressed them and were filled with the Holy Spirit. When the church met it was the presence of God in our meetings that attracted people. We also cared for people, loving them, showing them acceptance – it would be a feature of what people would say when they came in that they felt welcomed and loved.

A woman, I'll call 'Jen', lived in Hedge End. One Sunday she arrived for the very first time at our morning meeting in the village hall. It was a precious time with the presence of God filling the hall. The worship just took off with wonderful singing and worship.

Many were deeply moved, some in tears. Gillian and I noticed Jen looking around at it all, so we went over to reassure and befriend her. Jen was fine. "I've never been in a meeting like this", she said excitedly. "God's presence is all around and these people here know God in a way I have always wanted to". We prayed with her and during the worship Jen met Jesus and was filled with the Holy Spirit in a powerful way.

Some months after this her husband Tony came to Jesus too. I called round once at his home to find him searching the Bible wanting to know the way to become a Christian. Three decades later Tony and Jen are still at the same church serving and worshipping Jesus.

Al and family

At the start of a Sunday Nativity service in 1983 the village hall two strong, young men walked in wearing motorcycle outfits and crash helmets, studded jackets, boots, the lot. We had never seen them before, no one knew them or had invited them, and we wondered what was going to happen! As the service proceeded, they joined in, appearing quite comfortable amongst all that was taking place. I went up to them at the end of the meeting. Nick was already a follower of Jesus and had brought along his younger brother Al, who was searching for the truth. After a brief conversation we knelt in the hall there and then and prayed. Al encountered Jesus and began to follow Him. He joined the church and became friends with my two sons.

We discovered that Al was a superb guitar player and singer and 30 years later he is still at that same church and involved in the worship. Al married our niece, Joanne, and they have three fantastic sons. In the months following, Al's two other brothers and mum and dad also started following Jesus.

During this time, we were not sure what the key was or what had set off this season of people coming to Jesus. Later we learned that

Al and my son Mike and a few others, went out most evenings around Hedge End and prayed over a three-month period. They would see visions and have deep burdens to pray about people and situations and cried out to God to pour His Spirit on the church. It felt as though they had been taken over and were out of their depth. Pete Light, the pastor at the time, met with them and described what was happening as a season of intercession. We wonder if these two things were linked.

Stephen

Stephen was in his early 20s when I first met him at Hedge End. He'd had a difficult childhood after his father left home when he was only 4 years old. His mother was badly affected by the end of the marriage and at times she could not look after Stephen. Stephen felt utterly rejected, unable to settle and had struggled both at school and at work.

One day cycling through Hedge End, he noticed one of our church adverts on a notice board. He came along the next Sunday and was overwhelmed at the welcome he received and the warmth of the people although he knew none of them. The enthusiastic worship and the presence of God he described as "Amazing" saying, "I've never experienced anything like it".

Stephen encountered Jesus and started following Him and joined the church within 3 weeks. He started to meet with me and four other men, walking around Hedge End praying for the area. What a surprise we had! It was as though Stephen had suddenly been set free. The power of the Holy Spirit stirred him, he began to pray out loud and then he led us in prayer. He couldn't stop praying. It was powerful stuff! He was never the same again, a new creation filled with the Spirit. To this day he worships and serves the Lord in a church in Southampton.

Sharing His love

One day I was walking along the Hedge End shopping centre when a young woman stopped me to ask the way to the Post Office. Her name was Jane and she began to tell me her life story as we walked towards the Post Office. She told me that she was from Manchester and down here staying with her sister for two weeks. "I've got to sort my life out", she said. "Everything has gone wrong and my marriage is in ruins". She told me all this – and we had only met 5 minutes ago! As I listened, I couldn't believe my ears as she went on to say, "Really I am here to find God. I think He is the only one who can help me with all my problems!" Jane had come to stay for a break, spend time with her sister – and to find God! She went on to tell me that she had visited cathedrals and abbeys – large churches of all kinds – but nothing! She had not yet found God there.

I said to her, "Jane, you've found him!"
"What, you?" she laughed.
"No, not me", I replied, "but I know Him well. He loves me and He loves you too. I'd love to tell you all about him".

We found the Post Office, then Jane came home and met Gillian, who prayed for her and led her to Jesus! We kept in touch by phone and letters, Jane went on with God, found a lively, caring church in Manchester and God restored her marriage.

A transference of power

We were asked to help and oversee some new youth leaders at Hedge End Community Church. One night there was a meeting held at our home and one of the young leaders began to experience the Holy Spirit for the first time. She began to shake and speak in tongues. I directed some of the young people to go and pray for her. As they walked over to her they also began to experience the Spirit and some were unable to stand up. People began to laugh or cry as the Holy Spirit touched them. Later one of the parents came to collect his daughter. I answered the door and ex-plained what was going on. "What!" said the man, "I want to see this!" and he burst into the lounge and had not got very far when he too fell under the power of the Holy Spirit, hitting our sofa first and ending headlong across the carpet.

It's not really about the outward, physical things like shaking or falling, it's about people encountering and being encountered by the Presence of God. Biblically and historically though, when the Holy Spirit comes some of these physical things seem to happen. In the Old Testament there are several stories concerning King Saul where he is in the vicinity of people prophesying and is affected by the Spirit resting on them. I saw that evening at that youth group that sometimes when the Holy Spirit rests on one person that those around them also receive and a sort of transfer-ence of power happens.

Shepton Mallet

In 1984 we attended a Christian camping conference at Shepton Mallet with many from our church at Hedge End. The vicar of a large Anglican church had sent a message to the conference leaders asking for them to send one of their speakers to visit. So, I was sent along and took my friends, Rob and Barry, along with me. I am not sure who the church was expecting – probably some big conference speakers, but instead they got a local government officer, a lorry driver and a housing officer. In actual fact, Barry was greatly used in the gifts of the Holy Spirit and Rob was a great prayer warrior and still is to this day.

The vicar, who must have been in his late 40s and was extremely well spoken, greeted us. He explained that he had experienced something of the Holy Spirit and gave us the freedom of the place.

We were met at the service by a man named Bert, who was im-maculately dressed in a light grey suit and blue tie and had white hair and was again very well spoken. Bert said that "I've never had a touch from God, I find it can be divisive." We were not sure at this stage what we were getting into!

About 80 people gathered and the meeting started and they used worship songs from Mission Praise books and then I spoke briefly on Acts 2 the day of Pentecost. From previous experience I had found some people were quite cautious about the Holy Spirit, so I explained that it was Jesus who was the baptiser. John the Baptist announced that Jesus was the one who would baptise us with the Holy Spirit and with fire. Rob and Barry then shared from their own personal stories about what God had done in them. Then we asked people to stand and invited the Holy Spirit to come.

Within 30 seconds the power of God came tangibly. Bert who we had met at the start, fell to the ground and was rolling about under the front pew. The vicar fell backwards and his feet went up in the air, his black gown flying up like a huge kite. Other people fell as we prayed for them, a lot of people couldn't stand and others wept as the presence of God filled the place. We finished by praying for healing for some people and the vicar thanked us as we left. We never forgot our visit and heard that the church carried on afterwards in the things of the Spirit.

Ken

Ken, aged 26 years, noticed a very real change in his young wife since she had joined our church. He came along to see for himself and was taken aback by the presence of God, the fervent praise and prayer and the warmth of the welcome he received. "I could never join a church like this", Ken said, "it would change my whole life". Three months later Ken did encounter Jesus, was baptised in water and filled with the Spirit. His life did change and many years later he is still worshipping the Lord at a church near Winchester.

We would often find that people responded to the presence of God at our services at Hedge End. In fact, I would often tell people there that if they could get people through the doors to a service the presence of God would do the rest. When the early church gathered in the Upper room the power and presence of God fell and they poured out onto the streets. Though some thought they were drunk it did not stop 3000 people being added to their number! It is telling that when the church was at its most extreme, a massive number of people responded to God.

CHAPTER FIVE: THE GIFT OF CHILDREN

Over the years Gillian and I have prayed for many couples that had been told for one reason or another that they could not ever have children. To date we have prayed for thirty-four couples that have had around fifty children between them! In some cases, we prayed just once with them, other times we prayed regularly for months, and in some situations, we added our prayers to those of many others who were committed to pray for them too.

The circumstances around my own birth

It was not a ministry we chose, it was something that just took off once we had received the Holy Spirit. Reflecting on the wonder of it one day, I recalled my own unusual birth circumstances. My parents had, had two daughters, then a third baby came along but this time my mother was seriously ill and almost died in hospital. There were serious complications: the baby, Margaret Rose, lived only 2 hours. My devastated parents were told by medical staff, "You must never have any more children. You could lose the next baby and your own life too".

A few years later, unexpectedly I came along. It was a difficult time for my whole family, particularly as World War II had started. A new baby was the last thing my parents wanted at this time, apparently what they really wanted a dog! But I was born without the slightest problem for my mother and I was perfectly fit and healthy.

I was christened at Bitterne Park Church of the Ascension. My father recalled that day that the Luftwaffe did a fly-past in broad daylight (they were really heading for the Spitfire factories just a mile away)!

How interesting then that thirty years later the Holy Spirit has used us to pray for many other babies to be born.

Here are a few examples:

An Amazing Family
In the mid 1980s Gillian and I had seen an anonymous heart-rending letter published in the local Echo Newspaper from a lady who lived in Hedge End and was unable to have children. The letter told how heart breaking it was for childless couples to have to go through appointment after appointment and keep getting knocked back. So moved, Gilly and I placed the newspaper on the table laid hands on it and prayed over it for the woman.

Six months afterwards our friends, Rob and Sylvia, brought some people who lived next door to them to church. We were amazed to find out that it turned out that it was the same woman who had written that anonymous letter in the newspaper. About a week later, we met them while out walking and Gilly and I prayed for her. As we did, she declared, "that feels good, my head's hot!"

For twelve months after that, a group of us prayed for them regularly for her and her husband to have children. Their journey had taken years, including seeing many doctors, specialists, hospitals, clinics, and ended when their extended family had clubbed together a £1000.00 to get them a consultation with a Harley Street specialist. Their final appointment with the consultant culminated in them being shown an X-ray and the Dr showed them her fallopian tubes, which were twisted out of all recognition. The prognosis was final – it was absolutely impossible for them to have children. Following all this they had given up having their own and had gone on to adopt two sons.

However, God had other plans. God graciously healed her and they went on to have two beautiful children to add to the children they had already adopted. I recall the day at church that they told me she was pregnant for the first time and as she did, she wept with joy. After the birth of her daughter, the National press covered the story detailing the account of a miracle birth. The family went on to foster dozens of children. In the end their home was filled with children!

Caroline

In the Social Services HQ office, we had a very efficient telephonist. The lines were so busy the job required a great deal of patience and tact. Caroline had all of those talents and more. She was around 28 years old and married but could not have children. One morning she arrived at work, sat down at the telephone switchboard and burst into tears. She was escorted to an interview room by two of the young ladies working nearby. It appears that just that morning a letter had arrived at her home: following a further series of tests, examinations and appointments the letter confirmed that she could not have a baby.

Later a female member of staff and I sensitively asked if we could pray for Caroline. Arriving at work ten weeks after that, Caroline came in beaming and full of joy. She was pregnant! In due course Caroline brought her lovely little girl in to work to show all of us. We had only prayed for her once at work although many times in our own homes.

A Couple from Wales

I had a phone call from Wales one day from a couple who could not have children. They had been given my name by some mutual friends and asked if I could help. Prayer and discussions revealed they had suffered some heart-rending family situations in recent years. I encouraged them to bring those family situations to God and to fill their house with worship. As we prayed the Holy Spirit moved! They conceived and a beautiful baby girl was born. Her photo stands on my mantelpiece!

CHAPTER SIX:
SPIRITUAL WARFARE
AND THE PRESENCE
OF ANGELS

In Southampton in the early 1970s, we were starting to see people experience the Lord. As well as those who were starting to following Jesus, being filled with the Holy Spirit or getting healed, we also saw others set free from demonic oppression.

One unusual event took place during a lunch break at my offices, near the Civic Centre. Melanie, a typist at my work, was desperately thin and struggling with an eating disorder. She was losing weight week by week. Her arms were so thin and she was worried about the condition, but just did not want to eat. A Christian colleague at work asked her if she had been prayed for at her church. "No, my church doesn't believe in those things", she replied.

However, she agreed to let us pray for her. The Holy Spirit showed us that there was a spirit of rejection, which we told to leave in Jesus' name. Melanie shuddered for a few seconds and then stood up. "I feel lighter somehow", she said. "I feel free".

We felt that now we should send her to the baker's shop in nearby Windsor Terrace and buy a large sausage roll! She did and ate it without any problems. Her appetite returned, her weight came back and she returned to full fitness. On telling her local minister he promptly warned her not to have anything to do with us again! I met Melanie years later and she never again had any eating disorders.

Numerous deliverances like this one followed all through the 1970s – too many to recount.

Addressing demonic spirits over the university

After the church had started in 1976, the leader, Tony Morton, became convinced that students on the university campus were being influenced by demonic spirits. He invited a couple of leaders down to the campus to pray. We turned up and walked around the boundaries of the campus praying, believing that we were 'tearing down strongholds', as we had learned after hearing teaching on spiritual warfare.

Tony commented, "I think we've shifted a few things tonight, bro!"

I went home to bed. At the time Gilly and I slept in our converted attic at the top of our bungalow. Around midnight I awoke with a shocking sense of fear and I could hear like the sound of chain mail and someone coming up the stairs! I physically lifted Gillian to the other side of the bed to protect her and then walked to open the door. To my astonishment, coming up the stairs I saw a thick-set knight in black armour with a sword at his side, coming towards me slowly and loudly, helmet on and visor down. As unbelievable as this may seem, this was not a vision or something I was seeing in my mind's eye, the figure was actually there physically in my home. I shouted at the top of my voice, instinctively saying "Jesus!" As I did there was a blinding light and the figure completely disappeared.

In the morning I rang Tony and told him what had happened.

"That's amazing," he said and then he recounted how when he had gone to bed he and his wife, Hannah, were awoken when something heavy landed on their bed. There was a black panther on it. Tony called out the name of Jesus and also did a karate chop that went right through the panther and it too disappeared.

Tony went on to say that he had had another call from another of the church's leaders, who around midnight was awoken to see theatre-like masks with evil faces appearing and coming towards him. He said they were all in different colours and were hideous and it all stopped when he shouted out. Later he woke up and was running a high temperature and was sweating profusely.

After that time Tony reported a change for the better on the campus and that the demonic influence was gone.

Authority in the home
In the mid 1980s a doctor joined our church from the local surgery. One night he phoned and asked me to go and help him. A university friend of his had come over who had been involved in the occult and needed help. So, I went round to the doctor's house.

We prayed for his friend and tried to bind things, and drive any darkness out, but after forty-five minutes nothing seemed to happen. It was then that the doctor said, "Wait a minute, God has just shown me something!" I was relieved, because God hadn't shown me anything! He went on, "God has shown me that this is my house and I have authority over this house, and any visitor who comes into it, and (addressing the demon) I have authority over you, you foul demon, you cannot stay here, I demand that you leave!"

At this point the man being prayed for shuddered all over and stood up and a dark, shadowy figure, which was the same size and dimensions of the man, literally came out of him walked out of the open lounge door, into the hall and went out straight through the front door. The man was set free! I never forgot the lesson about having authority over your own home.

Forgiveness defeats oppression

When we were at Hedge End Community Church a woman came to visit for the first time. She didn't know Jesus and so when the Holy Spirit was visibly touching people in the hall, I went over and see if she was all right with it. She was ok and said, "I can really sense something is happening here."

Later that week we met her at her house. She started following Jesus and joined a house group in Botley. Sometime later, her husband had a word with me, saying how good it was what had happened to his wife but he said she still needs some help as she had had a troubled past and was damaged from it. So, Gillian and I arranged to visit them at home. The woman explained that she felt like she had these inner demons that spoke negative thoughts to her, so we started to pray.

We had not been praying long when a deep manly voice came from the woman saying, "We will never come out of her, she won't forgive them!" Her husband looked alarmed at what was happening. I addressed the evil spirits, "You've given yourself away, you've told us what's wrong and if she forgives people you've got no handle here and you'll have to go."

The woman then explained the pain she had had in the past and how she had made a vow, saying, "I will never forgive certain people." So with our encouragement she decided to forgive and began to call out loudly and urgently, "I forgive them" and she named the individuals who had hurt her. The demonic presence came out of her straight away with a loud roar in a deep voice, and she was free. I saw that day the importance of forgiving others and not giving the demonic a landing strip into your life.

Entertaining Angels

In 1978 we attended the Dales Bible week up in Yorkshire with other new churches like ours all over the UK. As strange as this sounds, throughout the week people had been reporting angelic visitations. There were lots of stories of angels walking with children back to their tents on the campsite and of angels having conversations with people queuing up for groceries!

One day that week, the organising committee received complaints from surrounding homes that at midnight and 1am the night before, singing was going on. However the meeting had finished around 9.30pm and no one had been gathering to worship. They also started to get reports on site about the singing and people could only conclude it had been angelic worship that was being heard!

Another evening that week, when Bryn Jones was due to speak, the worship time that night went right through the roof, it was Spirit filled and full of the presence of God. As it came to an end there was a wonderful crescendo of praise with 7000 people singing out in tongues – it lasted about 5 minutes. As it died down, there came a roll back of sound from both ends that met in the middle, like a wave. The sound was angelic, it was like being in heaven itself. People remarked afterwards about the incredible power and musicality of it. Bryn Jones got up to the microphone and said "Brothers and sisters that final roll-back came from heaven, those of you on the left thought it came from the right, those of you on my right thought it came from the left, it came from above, it was angelic worship you just witnessed."

Another day I had left our caravan to go and buy bread and milk and could hear beautiful singing coming from the stands at the site. I saw another person I recognised from another church nearby who could also hear it and remarked to him "Have they got tapes on?"

"No," he replied "I've heard it before, its angelic singing."

On the drive home down the M1, after that week, Gillian and I and our three children all heard the sound of angelic singing from inside the car. We checked the radio was off and the windows were all tightly closed. It was not the wind outside, the radio or the movement of the car. We listened for about ten minutes to a huge heavenly choir singing melodies that rose and fell as we drove along in amazed silence. It sounded strangely distant yet really close, just above the car! We all heard it and remember it still.

Divine protection

I know that we can all go through difficult situations, illnesses and accidents, but sometimes we can experience supernatural protection too. I've heard of others who have had similar encounters, but here are a couple of my own.

One morning in 1974, I was on my way to work in Southampton City Centre, driving from my home in Bitterne Park. I went down Bullar Road in Bitterne and stopped at a red light. I was first in the queue and pulled off as the light went green. I was three quarters of the way across the road to turn right, when suddenly, inside the car, something resembling a miniature white 'Corgi' toy van appeared in front of my eyes on the dashboard! It floated left to right across the steering wheel and out of the passenger window!

I was so shocked that I instinctively slammed on the brakes, bringing my car to a sudden halt. I stopped just as a real white transit van drove straight across in front of me, missing my car literally by a few centimetres. With the speed the van was going, If I had carried on driving it would have smashed into my car for certain and may have even turned it over several times. Stunned, I drove on to the next set of lights and it sank in that God had intervened and saved me and others from a terrible accident.

On another occasion, I was walking down Archers Road in South-ampton from the Social Services Area office where I worked. I was on my way to a client in Carlton Road. I noticed a young man coming down the road on the opposite side to me. I knew of this young man; he had been in our offices several times and caused a great deal of trouble. He was a violent man and well-known to the police. He was clearly in a distressed and agitated state as he came down the road kicking fences and threatening people.

When he saw me, the man crossed the road and came angrily to-wards me. I had nowhere to go and quickly prayed for God to help me. In that moment a tall, heavily built man was standing next to me. He looked like someone you wouldn't mess with! When the agitated young man saw him, he turned and gave us a wide berth before re-joining the pavement further down the road. I was in-credibly relived and thanked the tall man beside me. "You turned up just at the right moment" I said. The man just nodded and smiled.

I carried on about twenty metres before it hit me, "where had that man come from?" I turned back but the road was completely empty! He could not have reached the end of the road by the time I turned, there was nowhere for him to have gone. He just van-ished! It dawned on me then I had been helped by an angel.

CHAPTER SEVEN:
NEW LIFE CHURCH
AT WEST END

Mervyn and Joan Houghton ran a business in the city and loved the Word of God. They had longed for a local church in West End and gathered together a group of about fourteen people. I had agreed to help out for the first couple of years to get a church off the ground.

We started meetings in the Parish hall in West end in December 1991. It was a very informal sort of church and for six months we made slow and steady progress, but then in August 1992 the Holy Spirit seemed to come in dramatic ways, many people would fall down in the meetings. On occasions people even ran out into the car park because of the presence of God in the meeting hall.

We once invited a friend of ours to a meeting and being a bit nervous about it all she said that she didn't want any "fireworks!" However, during the meeting, after some prayer, God touched her she fell to the ground and the next day she felt so full of God she went out and immediately brought a friend to Christ.

During that time we saw many people set free from demonic oppression and many filled with the Spirit. Once a week a group of young people from the church met in a home in West End high street. As they prayed one night, they were all filled with joy and broke out into uncontrollable laughter. This was one phenomenon we would sometimes see as God interrupted our meetings. Struck by what was happening one of the young men telephoned Mervyn, and whatever it was they had, transferred to him and he also broke out into laughter! In fact, it so affected him that he couldn't get to sleep and ended up shutting himself in the garden shed in fits of laughter!

Our numbers went up from 14 to 20, to 66 people and when we held several open meetings on Sunday evenings 200 people came to see what was going on. People often recall the Toronto Blessing in 1993/94 that spread across the UK but we all experienced something before that in 1992!

The church we started then has since undergone several leadership changes but still meets today in the parish centre nearly 30 years later, as a Catalyst church (formerly NFI). Mervyn's original desire for a local church in West End has been realised.

CHAPTER EIGHT: DIVINE APPOINTMENTS

Sometimes it seems we walk into situations with people that seem to clearly have God's hand all over it. Someone once described that as a divine appointment. Here are some of my examples of divine appointments.

Mohammed the taxi driver

In 2019 I arrived at the Royal South Hants Hospital for a check-up following a minor operation on my eyes. There was nowhere to park the car, so I cruised around Lyon Street / Graham Road (possibly not a good idea in that area!) searching for a space. Suddenly a young man walked out in front of my car with his arms raised for me to stop. He was a handsome young man named Mohammed. He had noticed me driving round and asked what I was looking for. I explained the hospital appointment and my need for a parking space. He said, "You can have my space, but please help me. My car will not start". He showed me his large, silver taxi. "I must be in Winchester in 30 minutes", he said anxiously.

I tried to help. He produced jump leads and we connected them to our batteries, but nothing happened. Then I realised this was a divine appointment! "Mohammed, I believe God has sent me here to help you", I said, "He has sent me to show you his love for you".

Mohammed was shocked. "Oh my God!" he said, "What will you do?"

We disconnected the jump leads and I put hands on the car bonnet. I prayed loudly that God would start the car and show Mohammed his love (I did not tell him that this was the 4th car I had prayed for over some years, and God had started them all). Mohammed jumped in, turned the ignition key and the engine burst into life! He was shocked. "Oh my dear God!" he cried out. Then, to my surprise he got out of his car and gave me a huge hug! I told him about Jesus, then he set off for Winchester at great speed. Mohammed will never forget that encounter and what God did for him.

A story of Provision
God always blesses our giving of every kind. I have many examples where financial giving has brought wonderful blessing from God in most unexpected ways. I was in a meeting once in Netley, Southampton, one Sunday. The worship time was just beautiful. About 30-40 of us from all different churches had gathered to worship and pray for the area. I stood next to a young man I had never met before and as the worship came to a close, I felt strongly that I should speak to him.

Prompted by the Holy Spirit I asked him, "Do you have a financial need at the moment?" He was shocked, covering his face with his hands. We sat down and he outlined the situation. "To complete 2 years at Bible school I need £2000 within 2 months. I haven't got any of it". The money was needed to pay all the college fees.

"Well," I replied, "God knows. He has told me to empty my wallet of all the notes and cash and give them to you. This will be the start of God's provision". My wallet contained £49 in notes and cash, which he received somewhat reluctantly.

"How will you manage?" he asked.

"I'm fine", I said. "I have enough money at home, but this is so important. Go back to your church, to your college, anywhere you are to minister and tell this story but don't mention my name". He was astonished but did exactly as I had told him.

About four weeks later Aaron and his wife turned up again at Netley. He related excitedly that God's gifts had poured in as he shared. Not only had the total reached the sum he needed but an extra £200 had arrived from other churches and friends. He completed his course and moved into ministry in Bristol. How God loves to provide for all our needs and bless us in the most unexpected ways.

Healing in the restaurant
I was sat at the Inn-on-the-Sea café one lunchtime, at Lee-on-the-Solent. A young lady in her 30s came in with 3 children aged 7, 5 and 3 years. They sat at the table next to me. The children were very well behaved, and as I got up to leave, I remarked to the lady how good they were.

"Thank you", she said, "I was hoping they would behave well – they are all unwell with asthma".

"Can I pray for them?" I asked. She was surprised but readily accepted the offer and asked me to pray for her too because she too had long-term asthma problems. So, there in the café we prayed. No one seemed to mind at all.

"I do believe in God", the young lady said. "All our children have been baptised". Her husband was a Royal Navy Officer.

About six weeks later I was walking on the beach at Lee-on-the-

Solent again when the same woman and the children ran up to me, excitedly announcing that they were all healed of asthma. I linked them up with a local church and still look out for them when I'm in 'Lee'.

Haden

I was struggling to find the right telephone in Currys/PC World at Hedge End. I looked out for assistance and found a young man ready to help. He was South African and had long dreadlocks and a huge smile. After some discussion I purchased a telephone then gave the young man a booklet about Jesus. He listened carefully to the Bible verses I shared with him. Then he told me that he used to go to King's Church at Hedge End and that his mother was still a member there. "In fact", he said, "she said all the things you've said to me only last week. I guess it's time for me to return!" He said all this with a huge smile.

Wounded Healers

Although we witnessed many remarkable healings over the years, God chose to call my beloved Gillian to Himself at the age of 69 years. It all started with a sudden and totally unexpected heart attack in 2001. Three minor strokes followed resulting in brain cell damage and vascular dementia. She remained calm, at peace, in touch with Jesus all through the next 10 years until she was finally called home in August 2011.

Gillian's last 15 months were spent at a wonderful nursing home in Bitterne. The staff were just superb: efficient, caring and loving. And God moved by His Spirit there. During those 15 months we saw staff and visitors come to the Lord, others restored and some healed.

Cecilia was a senior nurse. What a wonderful person she was, totally committed to the residents and other staff, so attentive, helpful, and encouraging to the many visitors who came in to see their loved ones, some daily. I noticed that Cecilia limped badly and when I asked her how this had happened, she explained that 20 years earlier, whilst working at a hospital, she attempted to save a man who was falling backwards. She took most of the weight, injured her back badly and was off work for 6 months. "In fact," she said, "the pain has never left and I have not been able to sleep well due to the acute pain".

With Gilly's help, I prayed for Cecilia. She had one leg shorter than the other and when we prayed, her shorter leg grew instantly and she let out a scream: "What is this?!" I assured her it was Jesus. To her amazement she walked along the corridor without pain. Three days later she returned on duty radiant, announcing that she had slept so well without pain for the first time for many years, now no short leg, no limp, no pain!

Cecilia bought a new Bible, began to pray and told me that as a 10 year old girl she had stood on a beach, looked out to sea, asked God to let her serve Him and help people. The news quickly spread through the nursing home staff; now several called into Gillie's room for prayer and a number of real encounters took place there!

At this same nursing home worked a young man from the Philippines, Dave. He and his wife had received treatment and tests for 12 years but could not have children. His wife was now 41 years old, Dave 39. They were by now desperate. Dave heard about Cecilia's healing and asked us to pray for him and his wife. We did, just once, in the garden of the nursing home. Eight weeks later Dave rushed to tell us that his dear wife was pregnant! They went home to Manilla a few months later. I heard a year later they were attending a large Pentecostal church in Manilla with their new baby boy!

EPILOGUE: GO, TELL

The Gospel according to Mark, chapter 5, includes the dramatic story of Jesus meeting with the demonised man from the Gadarenes. Jesus set the man completely free and sent him back to the 'ten cities' area he came from with this instruction, "Go home to your own people and tell them how much the Lord has done for you, and how He has had mercy on you." (Mark 5:19 NIV). The man had been nothing special! In fact, he had huge problems, but an encounter with Jesus changed his whole life. His assignment was to go and tell what Jesus had done for him.

In a similar kind of account, Jesus meets with a Samaritan woman at Sychar. She was the woman at the well (John 4). She too was an ordinary person, with a very challenging past! Yet an encounter with Jesus changed her whole life. She too went back home to tell others; this led to many from the town coming to meet Jesus and they believed.

These accounts are of two very ordinary people (we don't even know their names!) but in encountering the amazing Jesus they were transformed. Jesus gave them a simple assignment – go and tell what I have done for you.

Gillian and I are very ordinary people. God gave us an assignment. It was not to travel to far off countries or even venture far from the south of England. We stayed local to Southampton and served

Him there. I stand amazed as I recall all He has done, for He has done it all, to Him be all the glory. You too have met with Jesus. You may think you are ordinary, but Jesus has given you that same assignment: Go and tell!

Let Your Glory Fall

In 1990 I was a delegate at a conference in the Brighton conference centre. The teaching that week was all about moving in the power of the Holy Spirit. There were about 3000 attendees and the worship time was incredible. During one of the worship times, the main speaker announced that, "The glory of God is descending upon this place."

At the time I was standing at the back of the auditorium near the doors. I looked up, and to my amazement, all across the ceiling along the front of the auditorium I could actually see a wonderful cloud. It is difficult to describe but it was white and yet gold, it billowed and seemed to have a life of its own. It was huge, silently filling the ceiling and gently moving. The speaker was saying the glory was going to land on the right-hand side of the auditorium first. I watched this happen! The cloud moved across and down, and as it landed it came among the people standing there, worshipping. Many crumpled down onto the floor. Some of those sitting down in that area fell off their chairs onto the floor and people were letting our cries of joy. The cloud then moved to the middle section of the auditorium and then to the left of the room. Each time the same things happened. As the cloud moved people responded. There were tears, laughter and joyful cries. In the meetings that followed many testified about the wonderful things that had happened at that service.

I saw all that happen from my position at the back and watched avidly. I remember at the end saying to God, "That's so wonderful Lord, but I never got touched at all!" I was almost questioning God about leaving me out, but He spoke to me as clearly as He has ever done before or since, and He just said, "I wanted you to see my glory". I went out the back of the auditorium afterwards and wept at what I had been allowed to witness.

At church we sometimes sing that song "Let Your glory fall", a wonderful anthem by David Ruis from a Vineyard church in Canada. I often wonder what people imagine when we sing that, whether they would believe it if I told them what I had seen that day and what the glory falling down on us would actually mean. In Exodus, we read that a pillar of cloud led God's people. My heart is to see the glory of the Lord descend again. It is my dream for our church in Southampton that God would fill it again with people, and one day when I asked the Lord to do that He said "But first I want to fill it with my glory!"

Yes, Lord, let Your glory fall!

ENDNOTES

With many thanks to David Payne who encouraged me to write all these stories and typed up the original draft. Thanks also to Jamie and Mike for helping me put this altogether.

More copies of this book can be ordered direct through Amazon.

Printed in Great Britain
by Amazon

57092004R00033